Book 2a

THE D
WORDS   ⎯⎯EME

We do
Lockdown

Written and illustrated by
MIRIAM ELIA

PUBLISHED BY
Dung Beetle Ltd © 2020
Created and printed in complete germ-free isolation

Dung Beetle Learning

What is a child beyond a carrier of germs and disease? How does one best structure and mould their vulnerable little minds, after Covid-19?

The answer is simple. All your family needs is this Dung Beetle guide, a large vat of bleach, and 24 hour exposure to media channels that broadcast death, disease and uncertainty into the comfort of your home.

In book 2a of the latest Dung Beetle guide, Mummy, Susan and John go through an indefinite period of self-isolation at home. During Lockdown the children will adapt to the 'new-normal' where they have no real life friends, no purpose, and most importantly no education beyond this book.

They will come to understand that a better world will only come when we bleach and destroy everything natural, and let FEAR control us.

The primary aim of Series 2 sees an emphasis on five areas of your child's development:

1. Safety- to become so risk aware, that they stop doing anything.
2. Control- that we can control nature, and not the other way round.
3. Caring- the kindest way to care is to cut yourself off from all humanity.
4. Entrusting- placing all of our freedom, without question, with scientists and politicians (who are advanced superior beings.)
5. Good intentions- basically justify anything.

This book belongs to:

Mummy has sealed us indoors.

"Coronavirus will kill us all!" says Mummy.

"But you said that about Climate Change last week," says John.

"Scientists predict this virus is going to kill most of the population," says Mummy.

"How do they know that?" says Susan.

"Because they are scared of what they don't know."

Mummy can't get a delivery slot.

"I will have to risk my life and go to the supermarket," says Mummy.

,

risk   averse   agoraphobia

We are shopping for emergency supplies.

"There is no lemongrass!" says Mummy.

"Oh dear!" says John.

"I'm starting to understand what life was like in World War II," says Mummy.

new words   exotic   food   shortage

The government have shut the church.

"I'm glad the church is shut," says Mummy.

"Why?" asks John.

"They use fear and guilt to control people."

"I'm heartbroken!"
says Mummy.

"We can't see Grandma
in person for at least
another three months."

"But we haven't seen
her since Christmas last
year," says Susan.

"When can we leave the house again?" asks John.

"When we have run out of toilet paper," says Mummy.

"How long is that?" says Susan.

"About 400 years," says Mummy.

new words   bog   roll   apocalypse

"I have just bleached the garden," says Mummy.

"But I thought Mother Nature is our friend?" asks Susan.

"Bleach is our friend now," says Mummy.

"What does the graph show?" asks Susan.

"If we stay at home forever we can be the exception to the rule," says Mummy.

Mummy has baked delicious cakes again.

"Eat up! The next daily death count goes live in ten minutes."

new words   death   comfort   bake

NUMBER OF DEATHS PER DAY IN THE UK

Total 41,347

The children watch the
old man on the ventilator
again.

"That's what happens if
you hug old people,"
says Mummy.

Susan starts to cry.

John's hands hurt.

"I have washed my hands over 100 times today, they are red and bleeding."

"Mummy says we have to defeat the virus at all costs," says Susan.

new words   obsessive   compulsive   disorder

"Why are we clapping every night?" asks John.

"Because our brave workers are at war with germs," says Mummy.

"And our neighbours can see us clapping."

Mummy is calling the police.

"Our council house neighbours have left their flat twice today. Their reckless behaviour is endangering our community."

It is 11pm. We are waiting in the car.

Mummy has gone to see her Scientist friend, to talk about Science.

"Will these days pass?" asks John.

"I hope not, I'm enjoying the feeling of total control," says Mummy.

Mummy is happy that the playground is still shut.

"We must be cautious, a germ might have gone down the slide."

Susan and John are sad.

"Shall we give him some money?" asks John.

"No, he doesn't take contactless," says Mummy.

new words   **keep**   **your**   **distance**

"Where are we going?" asks John.

"We are following the science," says Mummy.

Mummy has helped us see the world in a much safer way.

Now we know the park is just a hotbed of disease and infection.

new words

safe   grey   lives

New words used in this book

6 hazard / tape/ chaos

8 never / question / Science

10 risk / averse / agoraphobia

12 exotic / food / shortage

14 do / as / you're / told

16 when / it / suits

18 bog / roll / apocalypse

20 kill / everything / save / lives

22 suburban / safe / space

24 death /comfort / bake

26 original / sin

28 obsessive / compulsive / disord

30 evening / virtue / signalling

32 love / thy / neighbour

34 sexy / rule / breaking

36 despotic / misanthropic / existe

38 playing / is / hazardous

40 keep / your / distance

42 self / destruct / button

44 safe / grey / lives

Total number of new words 60

First published by Dung Beetle ltd 2020 © Miriam Elia